READ ME POETRY

Mr Grin and Mr Groan
And Other Conversation Poems

Acknowledgements

Every effort has been made to obtain permission to reproduce copyright material but there may be cases where we have been unable to trace a copyright holder. The publisher apologizes for any such error and will be happy to correct any omission in future printings.

"After Dark" © 1989 Michael Rosen from TEN GOLDEN YEARS. Reprinted by permission of Walker Books Ltd, London

"Nothing" © June Crebbin. Reprinted by permission of the author

"We're Breaking Up" (8 lines from "Schooling") from HEARD IT IN THE PLAYGROUND. © 1989 Allan Ahlberg, published by Viking

"The Wizard Said:" © Richard Edwards from WHISPERS FROM A WARDROBE, published by Puffin 1989. Reprinted by permission of The Lutterworth Press

"Mr Grin and Mr Groan" © Derwent May. Reprinted by permission of the author

"Tommy Hyde" from COLLECTED POEMS 1951-2000. © Charles Causley, published by Macmillan. Reprinted by permission of David Higham Associates

"Mrs Mason Bought a Basin" from OVER THE MOON. © 1985 Charlotte Voake, published by Walker Books Ltd, London

"Miss Antrobus" by Richard Edwards from TEACHING THE PARROT. Reprinted by permission of the publisher, Faber & Faber Ltd

"Me and Mister Polite" © 1994 Grace Nichols. Reprinted by permission of Curtis Brown Ltd, London, on behalf of Grace Nichols

"The Friendly Cinnamon Bun" © Russell Hoban, from THE PEDALLING MAN, published by Heinemann. Reprinted by permission of David Higham Associates

"Fishing" © John Agard from I DIN DO NUTTIN' published by Bodley Head. Reprinted by permission of Random House, UK

"Finding a Friend" © June Crebbin. Reprinted by permission of the author

"Puppy and I" from WHEN WE WERE VERY YOUNG. © A.A. Milne. Copyright under the Berne Convention. Published by Methuen, an imprint of Egmont Children's Books Ltd, London and used with permission.

"Puppy and I" by A.A. Milne from WHEN WE WERE VERY YOUNG by A.A. Milne, illustrations by E.H. Shepard, © 1924 E.P. Dutton, renewed 1952 by A.A. Milne. Used by permission of Dutton Children's Books, a division of Penguin Putnam Inc

"Don't Cry Caterpillar" © 1991 Grace Nichols. Reprinted by permission of Curtis Brown Ltd, London, on behalf of Grace Nichols

"How?" © 1986 Richard Edwards from THE WORLD PARTY. Reprinted by permission of The Lutterworth Press

"What Is Under?" by Tony Mitton from PLUM. © 1998 Tony Mitton, published by Scholastic Children's Books. Reprinted by permission of David Higham Associates

For Boris
M. C. S.

First published 2001 by Walker Books Ltd
87 Vauxhall Walk, London SE11 5HJ

2 4 6 8 10 9 7 5 3 1

This selection © 2001 CLPE/LB Southwark
Individual poems © as noted in acknowledgements
Illustrations © 2001 Mary Claire Smith

This book has been typeset in Adobe Caslon

Printed in Singapore

British Library Cataloguing in Publication Data:
a catalogue record for this book is
available from the British Library

ISBN 0-7445-6881-1

Mr Grin and Mr Groan
And Other Conversation Poems

Selected by Myra Barrs and Sue Ellis

Illustrated by Mary Claire Smith

WALKER BOOKS
AND SUBSIDIARIES
LONDON • BOSTON • SYDNEY

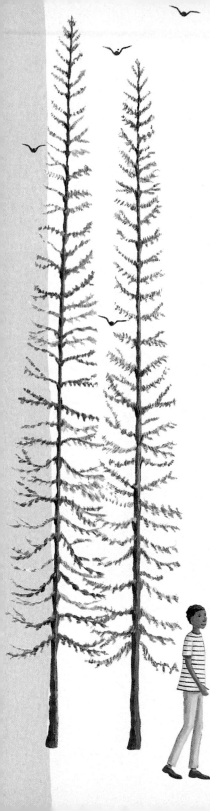

After Dark

Where are you going?
ROUND THE PARK.
When are you back?
AFTER DARK.
Won't you be scared?
DON'T BE DAFT.
A ghost'll get you.
WHAT A LAUGH!
I know where it lives.
NO YOU DON'T.
And you'll run away.
NO I WON'T.
It got *me* once.
IT DIDN'T – DID IT?
It's all slimy.
'TISN'T, IS IT?
Where are you going?
I'M STAYING AT HOME.
Aren't you going to the park?
NOT ON MY OWN.

Michael Rosen

LAZYBONES

Lazybones, let's go to the farm
    Sorry, I've got a headache
Lazybones, let's go pounding grain
    Sorry, my leg isn't right
Lazybones, let's go fetch firewood
    Sorry, my hands are hurting
Lazybones, come and have some food
    Hold on, let me wash my hands!

Traditional

NOTHING

What

did

you

say,

Kevin?

Nothing,

Miss.

Oh

really?

That's

clever.

I'd

like

to know

how

you

can

say

nothing.

It's

easy,

Miss.

Nothing

to it!

June Crebbin

WE'RE BREAKING UP

We're breaking up
The children shout
At breakneck speed
We're breaking out.

We're breaking down
The teachers said
We need a break
Breakfast in bed.

Allan Ahlberg

THE WIZARD SAID:

"You find a sheltered spot that faces south…"
    "And then?"
"You sniff and put two fingers in your mouth…"
    "And then?"
"You close your eyes and roll your eye-balls round…"
    "And then?"
"You lift your left foot slowly off the ground…"
    "And then?"
"You make your palm into a kind of cup…"
    "And then?"
"You *very quickly* raise your right foot up…"
    "And then?"
"You fall over."

Richard Edwards

MR GRIN AND MR GROAN

When Mr Grin and Mr Groan
Sat down at breakfast table
They both ate up the marmalade
As fast as they were able.

They heaped it up upon their toast
Until the pot was through.
Then Mr Grin said cheerfully
"I've had as much as you!"

But Mr Groan stared at his plate
And stiffly stirred his tea,
And looking *very* cross, he said
"You've had as much as me!"

Derwent May

Ferry Me

"Ferry me across the water,

　　Do, boatman, do."
"If you've a penny in your purse

　　I'll ferry you."

"I have a penny in my purse,

　　And my eyes are blue;
So ferry me across the water,

　　Do, boatman, do."

"Step into my ferry-boat,

　　Be they black or blue,
And for the penny in your purse

　　I'll ferry you."

Christina Rossetti

TOMMY HYDE

Tommy Hyde, Tommy Hyde,

What are you doing by the salt-sea side?

Picking up pebbles and smoothing sand

And writing a letter on the ocean strand.

Tommy Hyde, Tommy Hyde,

Why do you wait by the turning tide?

I'm watching for the water to rub it off the shore

And take it to my true-love in Baltimore.

Charles Causley

love

WHAT'S IN THERE?

What's in there?

    Gold and money.

Where's my share of it?

    The mouse ran away with it.

Where's the mouse?

    In her house.

Where's the house?

    In the wood.

Where's the wood?

    The fire burnt it.

Where's the fire?

    The water quenched it.

Where's the water?

    The brown bull drank it.

Where's the brown bull?

    At the back of Birnie's Hill.

Where's Birnie's Hill?

    All clad with snow.

Where's the snow?

    The sun melted it.

Where's the sun?

    High, high up in the air.

Anonymous

MRS MASON BOUGHT A BASIN

Mrs Mason bought a basin,

      Mrs Tyson said, What a nice 'un,

What did it cost? said Mrs Frost,

      Half a crown, said Mrs Brown,

Did it indeed, said Mrs Reed,

      It did for certain, said Mrs Burton.

Then Mrs Nix, up to her tricks,

      Threw the basin on the bricks.

Anonymous

MISS ANTROBUS

Why do you love your octopus,
Miss Antrobus, Miss Antrobus?
Why do you love your octopus,
Miss Antrobus, my dear?

I love my octopus because
It hugs me and it wriggles,
I love my octopus because
Its wriggles give me giggles,
I love my octopus because
It juggles jars of pickles,
I love my octopus because
It tickles, oh, it tickles!

Richard Edwards

ME AND MISTER POLITE

Again and again
we met in the lane.

We met in the sunshine
We met in the rain

We met in the windy
We met in the hail

We met in the misty
And autumn-leaf trail

On harsh days and dark days
On days mild and clear

And if it was raining
He'd say, "Nice weather for ducks"

And if it was sunny
He'd say, "Good enough for beach-wear"

And if it was windy
He'd say, "We could do without that wind"

And if it was nippy
He'd say, "Nippy today"

And if it was cold-windy-rainy-grey
(which it nearly always was)
He'd say, "Horrible day"
Or "Not as good as it was yesterday"

And he'd hurry away with a brief tip of his hat
His rude dog pulling him this way and that.

Grace Nichols

THE FRIENDLY CINNAMON BUN

Shining in his stickiness and glistening with honey,

safe among his sisters and his brothers on a tray,

with raisin eyes that looked at me as I put down my money,

there smiled a friendly cinnamon bun, and this I heard him say:

"It's a lovely, lovely morning, and the world's a lovely place;

I know it's going to be a lovely day.

I know we're going to be good friends; I like your honest face;

Together we might go a long, long way."

The baker's girl rang up the sale, "I'll wrap your bun,"

said she,

"Oh no, you needn't bother," I replied.

I smiled back at that cinnamon bun and ate him,

one two three,

and walked out with his friendliness inside.

Russell Hoban

FISHING

Fishing all day long
and can't catch a thing.

What's wrong? What's wrong?
I ask the little worm
at the end of my hook.

The worm give me one look
and start to sing this song:

"Fish like to slip
in deep rain
Not take a dip
in frying pan."

John Agard

FINDING A FRIEND

"Will you be my friend?"
said the rubbish to the river.
"No, never."

"Will you be my friend?"
said the spider to the fly.
"Not I."

"Will you be my friend?"
said the lion to the deer.
"No fear."

"Will you be my friend?"
said the boat to the sea.
"Maybe."

"Will you be my friend?"
said the child to the summer days.
"Always."

June Crebbin

PUPPY AND I

I met a Man as I went walking;
We got talking,
Man and I.
"Where are you going to, Man?" I said
  (I said to the Man as he went by).
"Down to the village, to get some bread.
  Will you come with me?" "No, not I."

I met a Horse as I went walking;
We got talking,
Horse and I.
"Where are you going to, Horse, to-day?"
  (I said to the Horse as he went by).
"Down to the village to get some hay.
  Will you come with me?" "No, not I."

I met a Woman as I went walking;
We got talking,
Woman and I.
"Where are you going to, Woman, so early?"
    (I said to the Woman as she went by).
"Down to the village to get some barley.
    Will you come with me?" "No, not I."

I met some Rabbits as I went walking;
We got talking,
Rabbits and I.
"Where are you going in your brown fur coats?"
    (I said to the Rabbits as they went by).
"Down to the village to get some oats.
    Will you come with us?" "No, not I."

I met a Puppy as I went walking;
We got talking,
Puppy and I.
"Where are you going this nice fine day?"
    (I said to the Puppy as he went by).
"Up in the hills to roll and play."
    "*I'll* come with you, Puppy," said I.

AA Milne

Don't cry, Caterpillar
Caterpillar, don't cry
You'll be a butterfly – by and by.

Caterpillar, please
Don't worry 'bout a thing

"But," said Caterpillar,
"Will I still know myself – in wings?"

Grace Nichols

How?

How did the sun get up in the sky?
– A billy goat tossed it up too high,
Said my Uncle.

How did the stars get up there too?
– They're sparks from the thunder-horse's shoe,
Said my Uncle.

And tell me about the moon as well.
– The moon jumped out of an oyster shell,
Said my Uncle.

And how did the oceans get so deep?
– I'll tell you tomorrow. Now go to sleep,
Said my Uncle.

Richard Edwards

What is under the grass, Mummy,
what is under the grass?
Roots and stones and rich soil
where the loamy worms pass.

What is over the sky, Mummy,
what is over the sky?
Stars and planets and boundless space,
but never a reason why.

What is under the sea, Mummy,

what is under the sea?

Weird and wet and wondrous things,

too deep for you and me.

What is under my skin, Mummy,

what is under my skin?

Flesh and blood and a frame of bones

and your own dear self within.

Tony Mitton

OTHER READ ME BOOKS

Read Me Beginners are simple rhymes and
stories ideal for children learning to read.

Read Me Story Plays are dramatized versions of favourite
stories, written for four or more voices to share.